DOUBLE BASS

TEAM STRINGS

CHRISTOPHER BULL
OLIVE GOODBORN &
RICHARD DUCKETT

IMP

International Music Publications Limited

Edited by BARRIE CARSON TURNER

Piano accompaniments by CHRISTOPHER BULL

Sincere thanks are extended to the following people:
ANN GOODBORN, Double Bass Tutor, Birmingham Schools Symphony Orchestra, for her invaluable advice on technical matters.
ANGELA GREGORY of Kings Norton Girls School, Birmingham, and all the pupils who worked on the material in preparation.

First Published 1993.

Cover Design: IAN BARRETT
Cover Photography: RON GOLDBY
Production: STEPHEN CLARK and MARK MUMFORD
Typesetting: Headline Publicity Ltd., Chelmsford, Essex
Instruments photographed are "Andreas Zeller" courtesy of Stentor Music Co. Ltd., Reigate, England.
Printed in England by Halstan & Co. Ltd., Amersham, Bucks.

TEAM STRINGS: Double Bass
ISBN 0 86359 989 3/ORDER REF: 18418/215-2-880

Team Strings Ensemble

TEAM STRINGS ensemble material has been specially written so that it can be played by almost any combination of string instruments the teacher may encounter.

On each ensemble page there are three parts. The first is the melody and the second is a duet part. The third is either a bass line, a harmony part or a descant. Each piece can therefore be used as a solo, duet, or trio, with or without piano accompaniment.

By allocating the parts to different instruments it is easy to create a considerable variety of mixed ensembles, from a simple duet to a full string orchestra.

In addition to this, each piece can be extended into a longer one by varying the textures in subsequent verses. This can be done by reallocating the parts, playing in unison, using *pizzicato* accompaniments, introducing solo passages, etc.

The following symbols have been used to provide an immediate visual identification:

 Pieces with piano accompaniment

 Ensemble page
(score included in ACCOMPANIMENTS book)

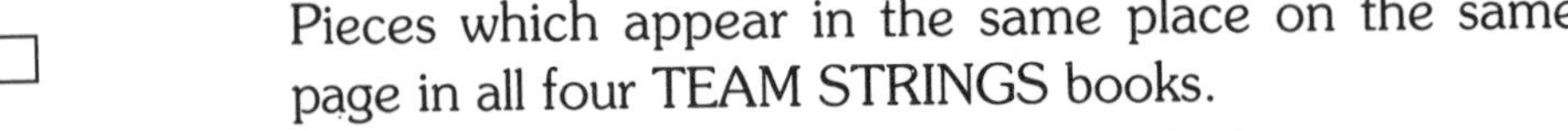

☐ Pieces which appear in the same place on the same page in all four TEAM STRINGS books.

Introducing Team Strings

The TEAM STRINGS series has been designed to meet the needs of young string players everywhere, whether lessons are given individually, in groups or in the classroom.

Musical variety

Each book contains a wide variety of musical styles, from the Baroque and Classical eras to Christmas carols, folk music, and popular favourites. In addition there are many original pieces, studies and technical exercises. Furthermore, TEAM STRINGS offers material for mixed string ensemble as well as solos with piano accompaniment.

Ensemble pieces

All TEAM STRINGS books contain corresponding pages of music which can be played together in harmony. Thus, even beginners are given early ensemble experience and the opportunity to share lessons with other players.

Every TEAM STRINGS book contains a supplement relating to the duets in TEAM WOODWIND for flute and oboe. There are also string parts which can be used in conjunction with TEAM BRASS, TEAM WOODWIND and TEAM PERCUSSION to form mixed instrumental ensembles.

National Curriculum & GCSE skills

TEAM STRINGS has been designed to help meet the requirements of the National Curriculum for music. In addition to fostering musical literacy, 'Rhythm Grids' and 'Play By Ear' lines provide early opportunities for composition and improvisation. This aspect of TEAM STRINGS can be a useful starting point for these elements in the GCSE examination course now followed by most secondary schools.

Comprehensive notes on the use of this series, scores of the ensemble material, piano accompaniments and approaches to creative music making are given in the ACCOMPANIMENTS book.

Supplementary Material

Parts are available for Brass, Woodwind, Recorder and Percussion which can be added to the TEAM STRINGS ensembles. Each piece can therefore be extended to incorporate a wide variety of additional instruments. These supplementary parts can be used for almost any combination of instruments from a small '*ad hoc*' group to full orchestra.

Wind, Brass, and Percussion parts for the Ensemble Pieces in TEAM STRINGS are available separately.

Lesson diary & practice chart

Date (week commencing)	Enter number of minutes practised.							Teacher indicates which pages to study.
	Mon	Tue	Wed	Thur	Fri	Sat	Sun	

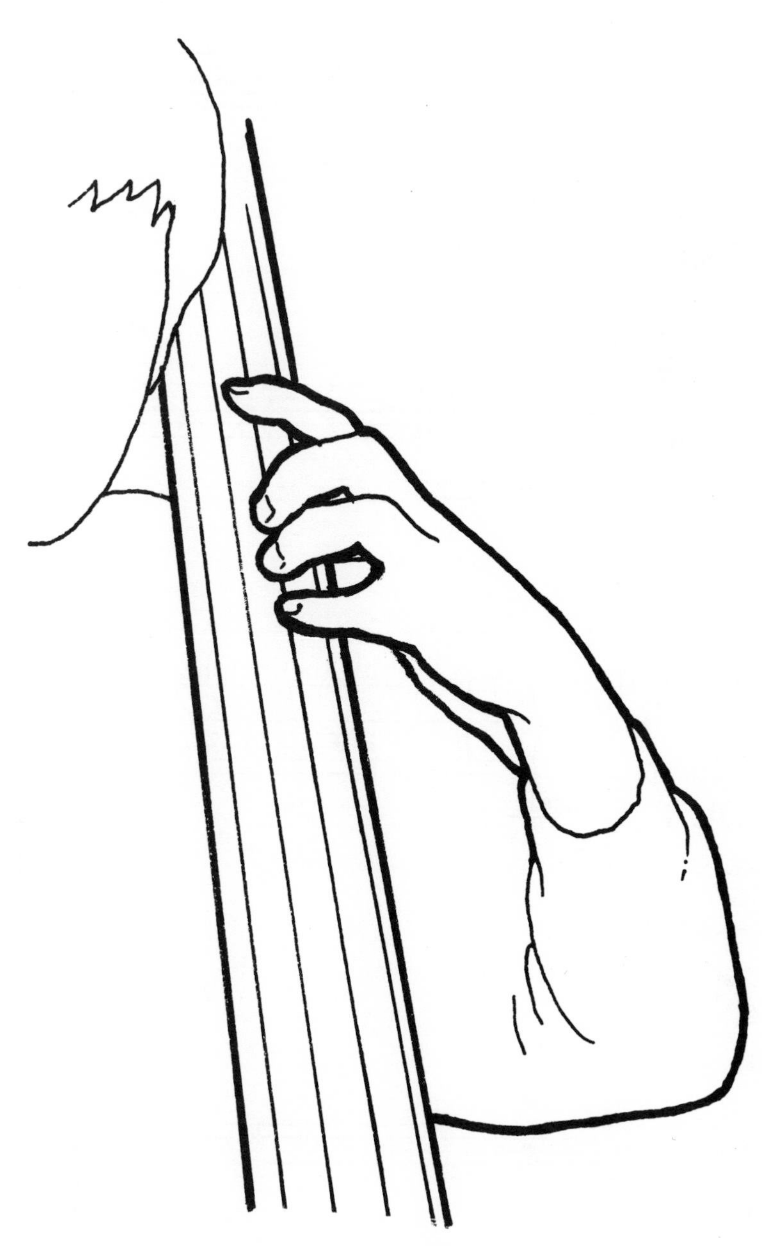

Start with D . . .

*French time-names may be used.

. . . then on to A

0
Clap, say, and play the rhythm
A CROTCHET REST lasts for ONE beat
Open A is written in the bottom space
BAR LINES divide a line of notes into sets. In 4/4 time each bar adds up to four crotchet beats
1+1+1+1= 4
2+2= 4

D and A together

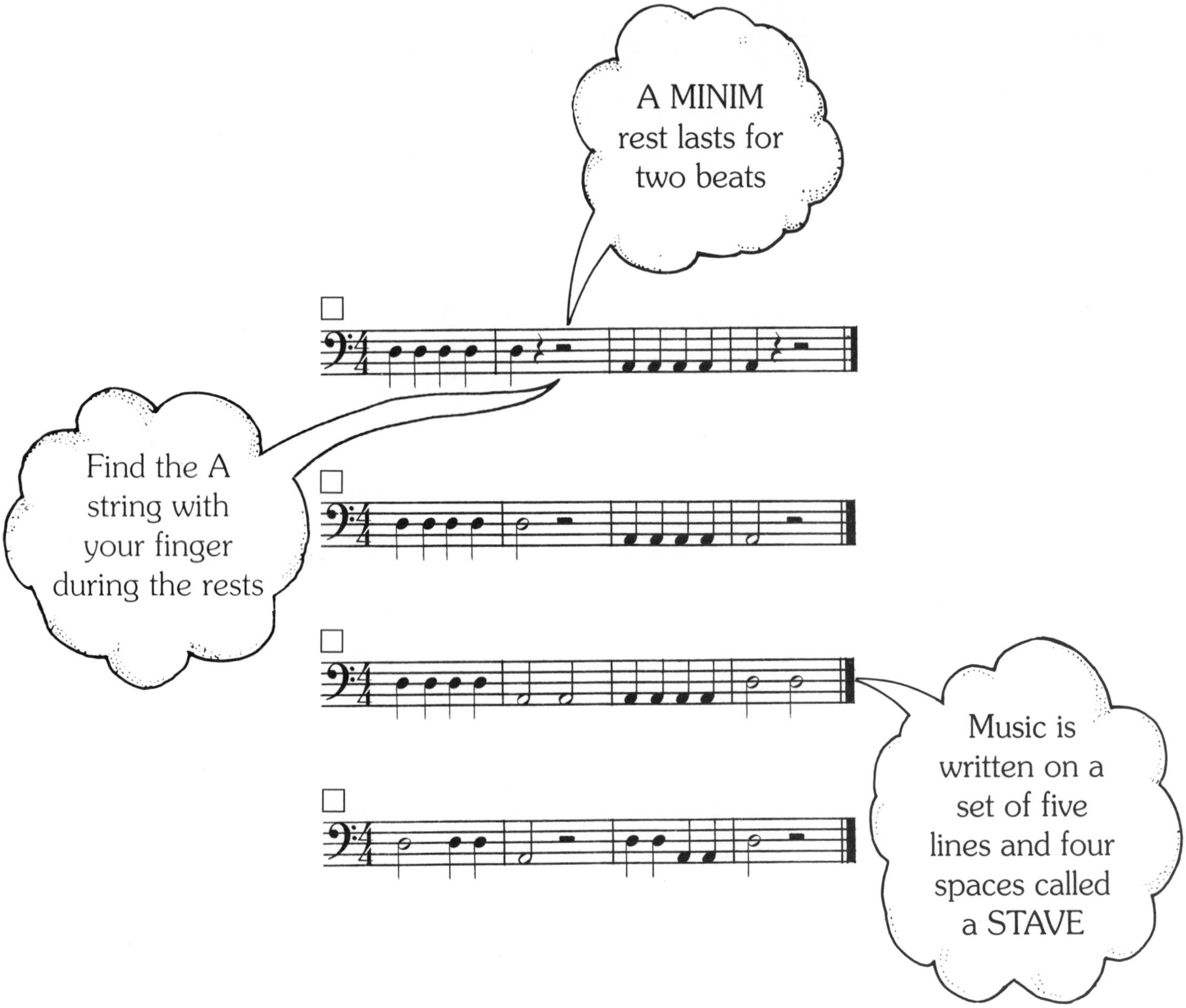

A MINIM rest lasts for two beats

Find the A string with your finger during the rests

Music is written on a set of five lines and four spaces called a STAVE

By the Rhine

This piece fits with *German tune* (page 23).

0
The note G
Music for the double bass always begins with the BASS CLEF
Open G is written in the top space
G and D together
A little march
Chiming bells
G, D and A

0
The note E
The small line below the stave is called a LEGER LINE
Open E is written on one leger line
A lively piece
All four strings
Try playing this piece with your eyes closed!
Barn dance
Starlight
This pieces fits with *Twinkle, twinkle little star* (page 27).

On the lake

This piece fits with *Flamingo* (page 12).

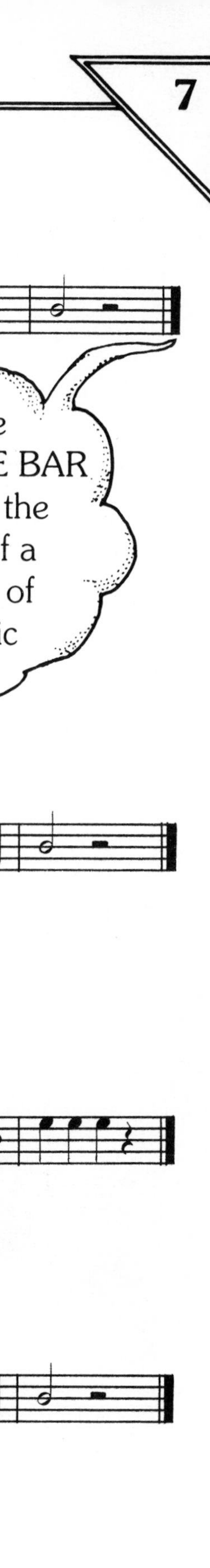
The
DOUBLE BAR
marks the
end of a
piece of
music

The traveller

This piece fits with *Tramping* (page 11).

The pendulum

This piece fits with *The clock* (page 17).

At dusk

This piece fits with *Now the day is over* (page 17).

Magic spells

This piece fits with *The wizard* (page 43).

Using the bow

Down bow

Up bow

ARCO means play with the bow.

PIZZICATO (or *pizz*) means pluck the strings.

From now on *everything* can be played *arco*, unless marked otherwise.

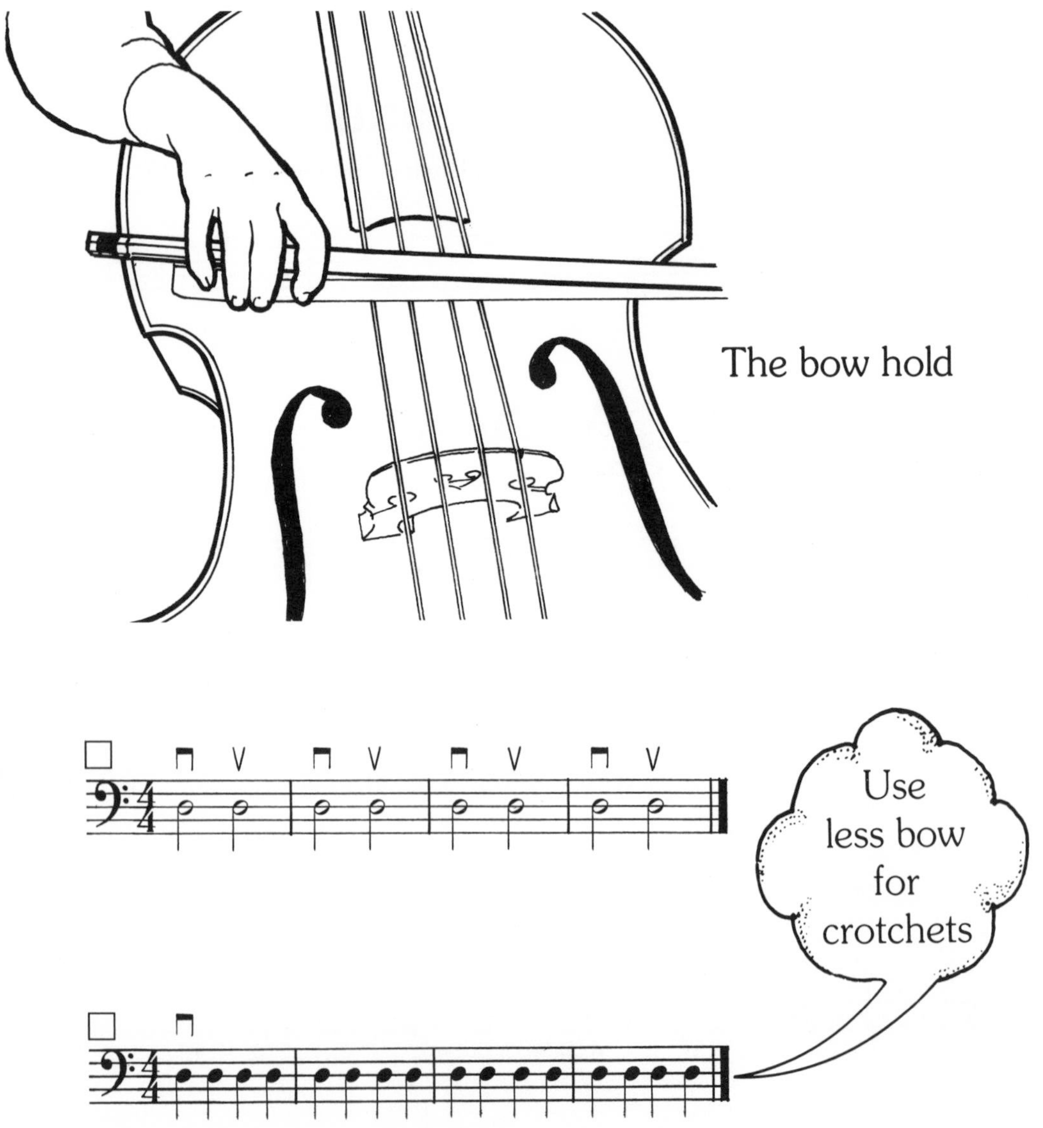

The bow hold

Use less bow for crotchets

Bowing exercises

Watch out for these signs
Always keep your bow straight!

■ The music on pages 2 - 7 can also be used as bowing exercises.

First finger E

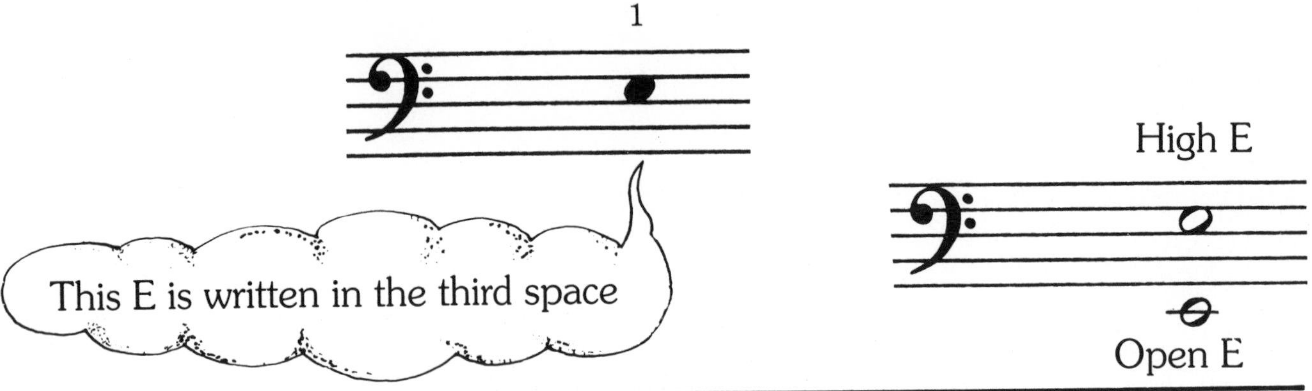
1
This E is written in the third space
High E
Open E

By the stream

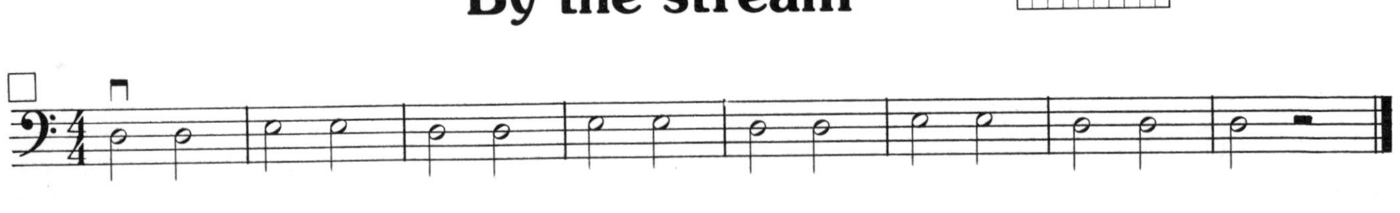

The night sky

This piece fits with *Twinkle, twinkle little star* (page 27).

Fourth finger F♯

4

This F sharp is written on the fourth line

V
Down bow
The sharp sign makes all the notes in the bar with the same letter name sharp

Tramping

Traditional

The shepherd

Bavaria

This piece fits with *German tune* (page 23).

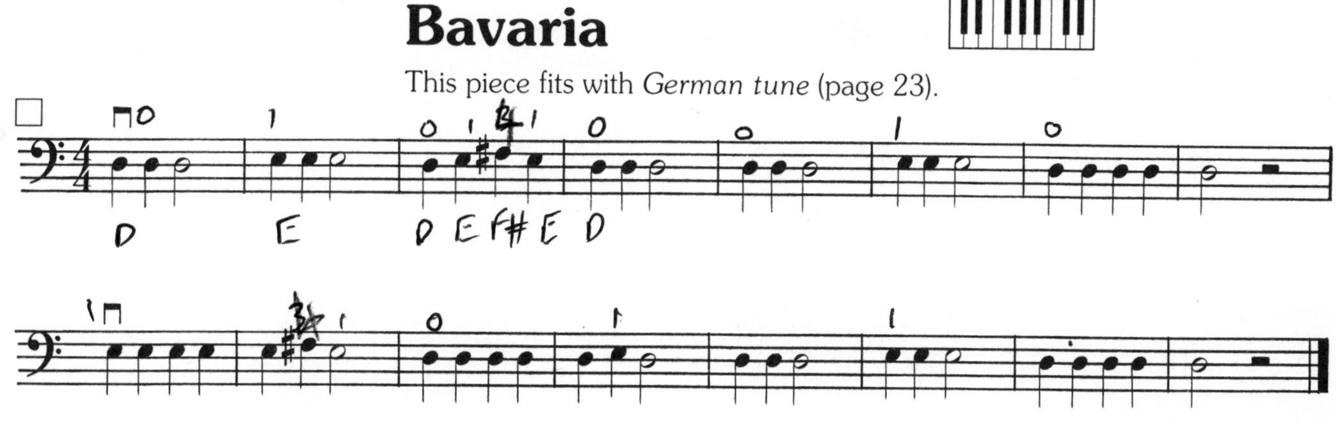

Flamingo

The magic carpet

This piece fits with *The wizard* (page 43).

Tunes using D E F♯ & G

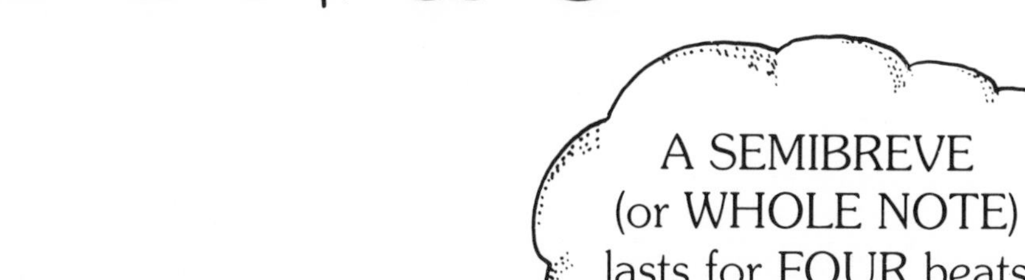
A SEMIBREVE
(or WHOLE NOTE)
lasts for FOUR beats

The piper

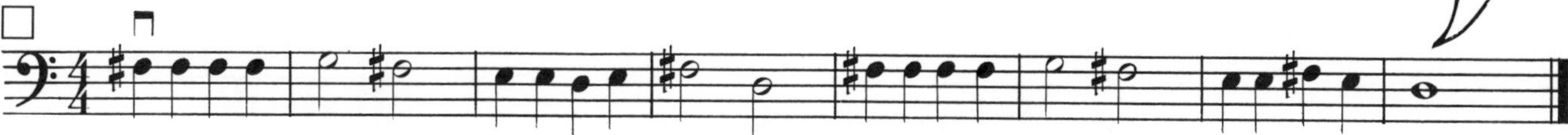

Lucy

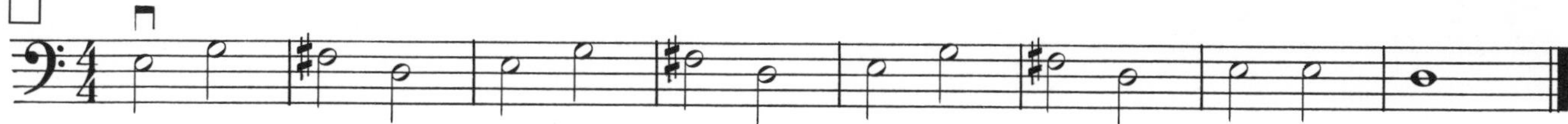

Folk song

Falling leaves

This piece fits with *Autumn* (page 21).

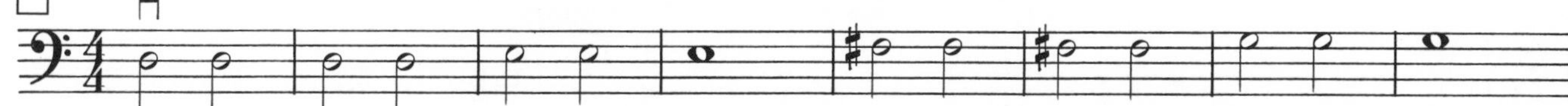

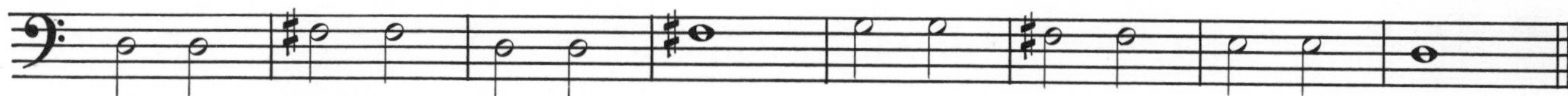

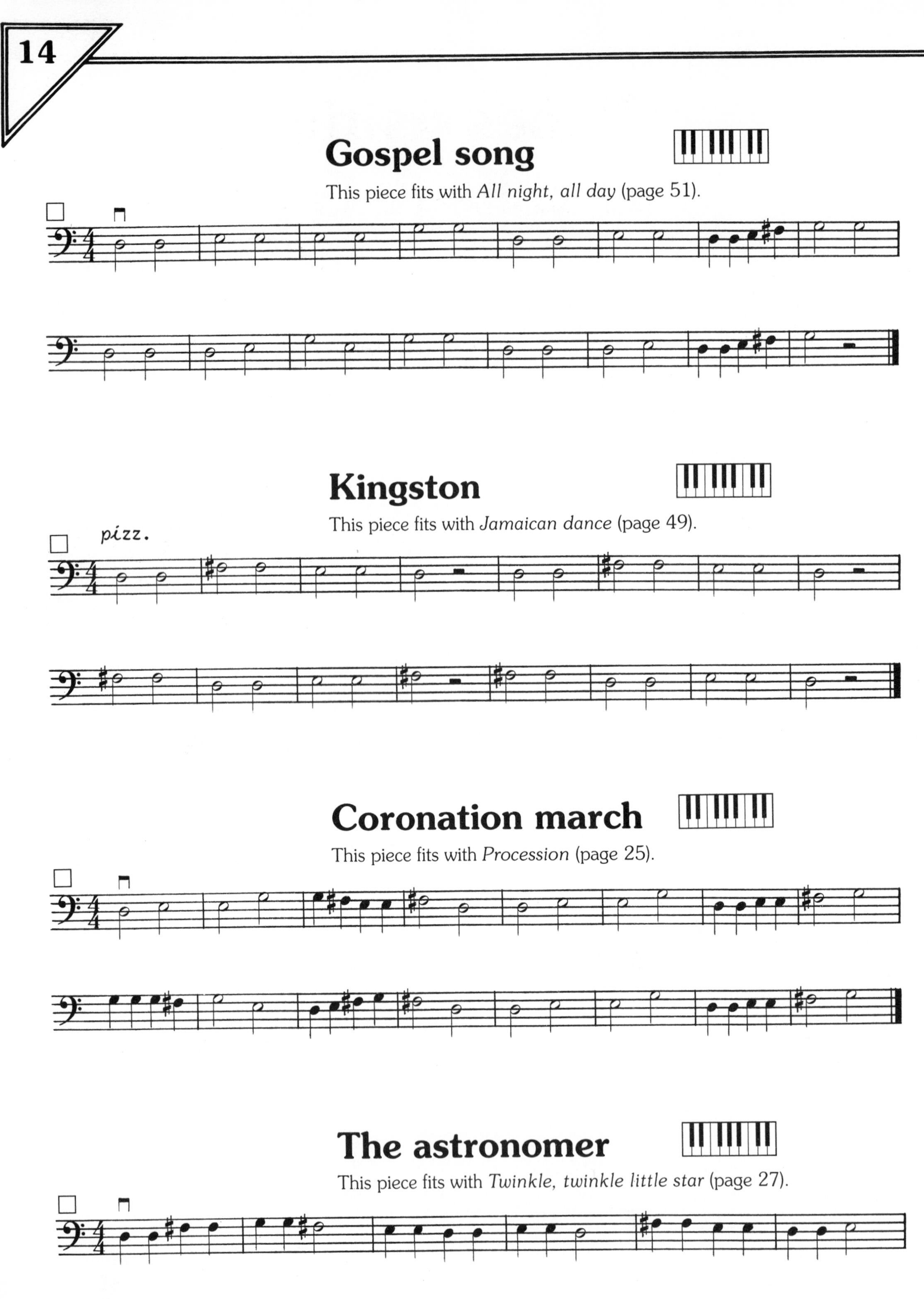

Gospel song

This piece fits with *All night, all day* (page 51).

Kingston

This piece fits with *Jamaican dance* (page 49).

Coronation march

This piece fits with *Procession* (page 25).

The astronomer

This piece fits with *Twinkle, twinkle little star* (page 27).

Notes on the A string

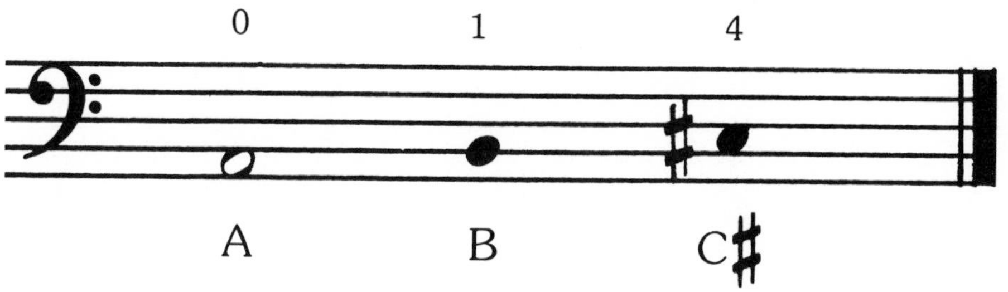

The harvest

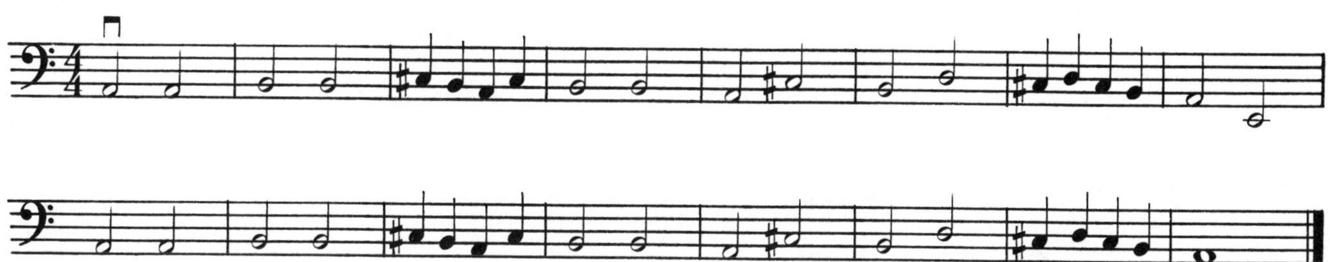

Au clair de la lune

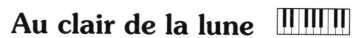

French traditional

Make up your own piece using the notes on the A string

Dance

Song from Holland

Chorale

Arden Leys

Quick march

The grasshopper

Notes on the G string

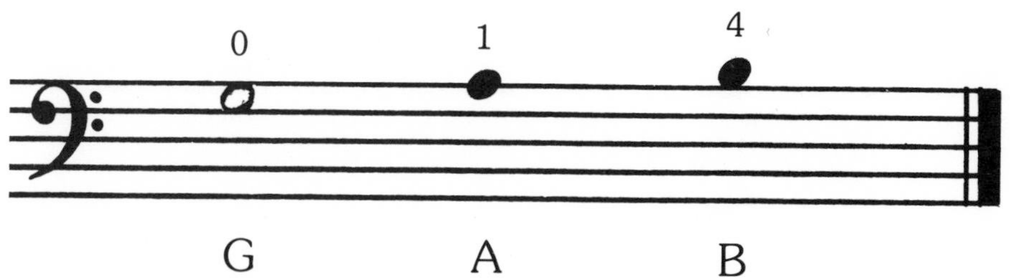

Merrily we roll along

Traditional

Tin soldiers

The clock

Now the day is over

S. BARING-GOULD (1834-1924)

The key signature of G

The key signature of D

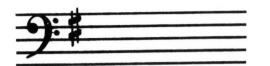

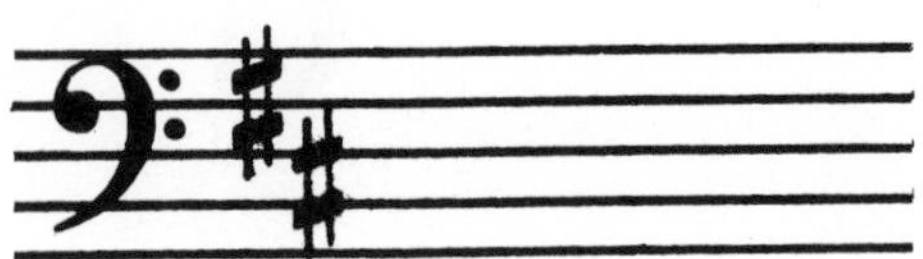

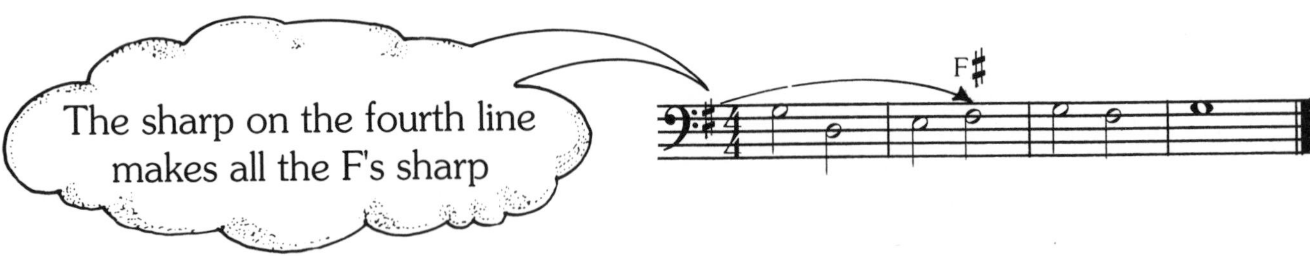
The sharp on the fourth line makes all the F's sharp
F♯

Promenade

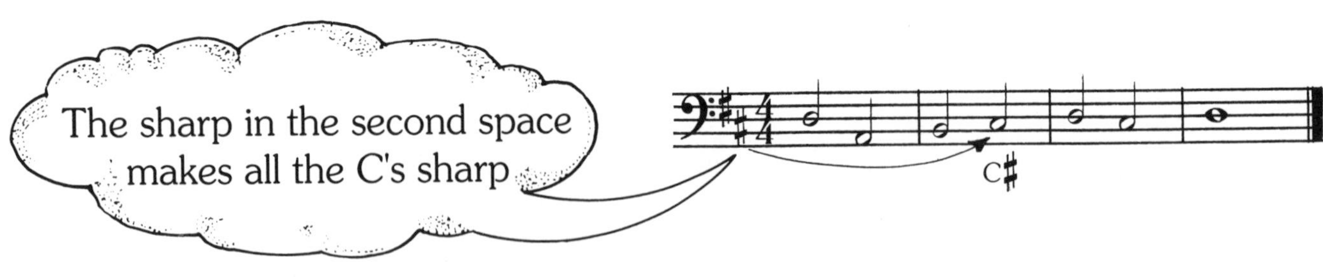
The sharp in the second space makes all the C's sharp
C♯

Daydreams

Five-note patterns

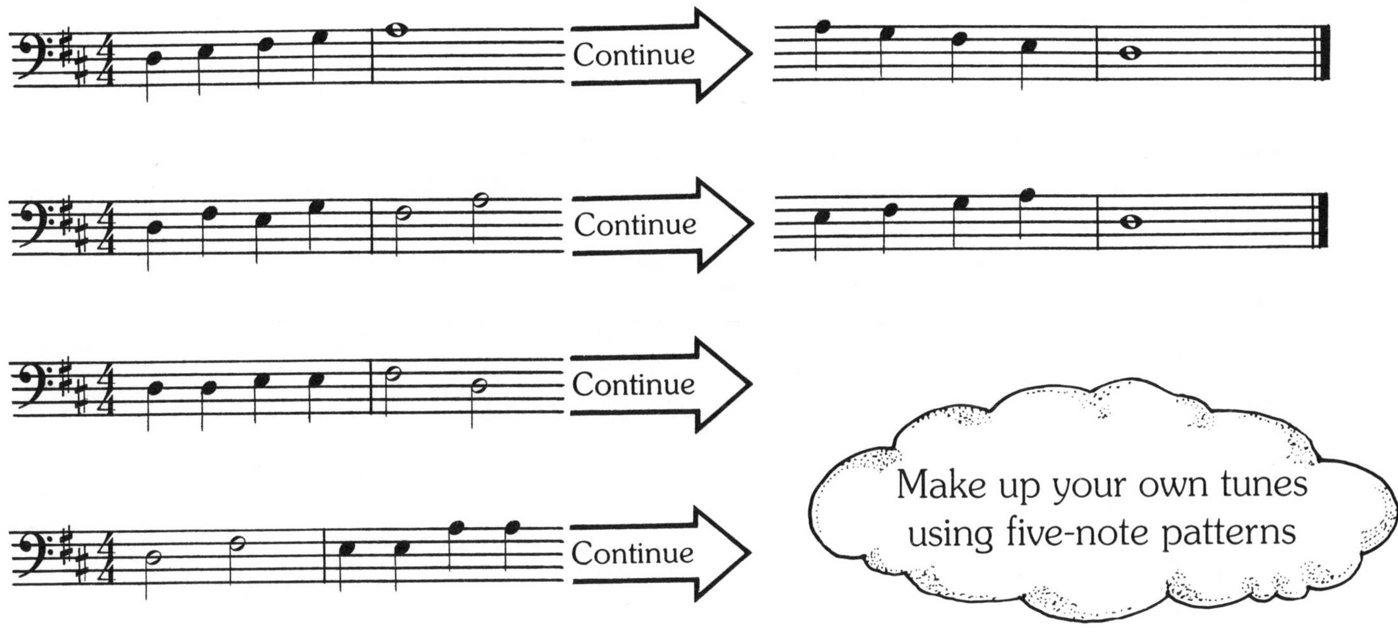

Mr Foster's round

Magnolia

The old man of Hoy

Notes on the E string

play by ear

Continue

Continue

Autumn

1.

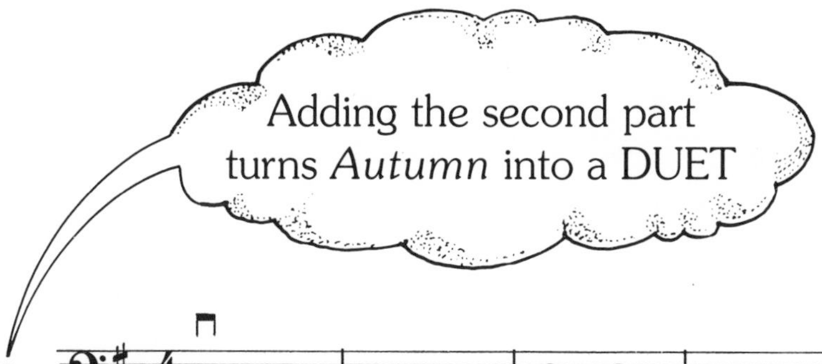

Adding the second part turns *Autumn* into a DUET

2.

All three parts played together make a TRIO

3.

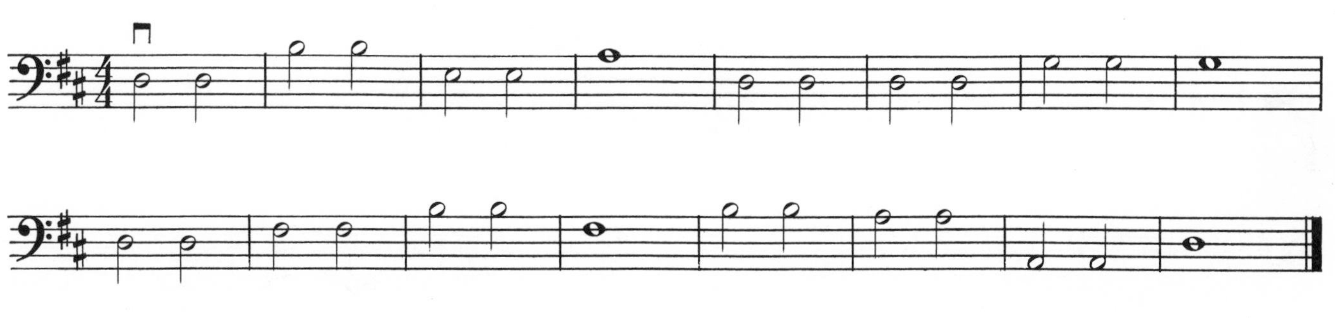

Dotted minims

A DOTTED MINIM
lasts for THREE beats
Count: 1 2 3

Sorrow

Rigaudon

HENRY PURCELL (1658-1695)

Arpeggios

Shady grove

American traditional

German tune

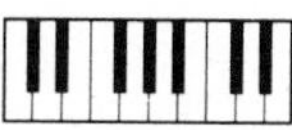

Traditional

1.

2.

3.

Quavers

Semibreve
1 (2) (3) (4)
Minims
1 (2) 3 (4)
Crotchets
1 2 3 4
Quavers
1 + 2 + 3 + 4 +

Each bar adds up to four crotchets

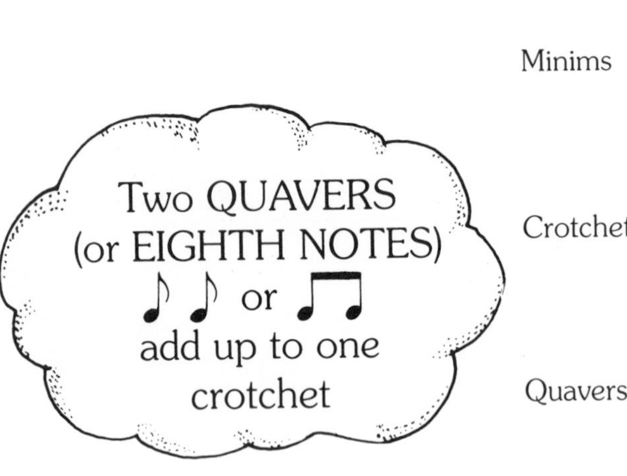
Two QUAVERS
(or EIGHTH NOTES)
or
add up to one
crotchet

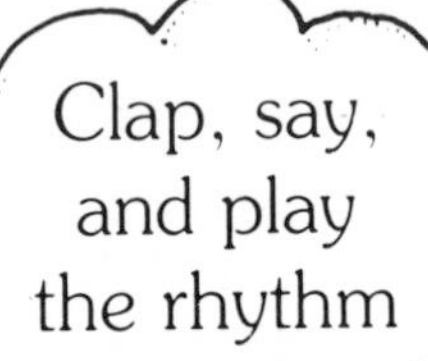
Clap, say,
and play
the rhythm

My goose

Round

(1)
(2)
The two dots mean that the music should be repeated
Who's that yonder?
Spiritual

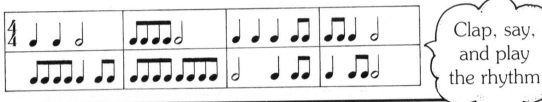

Procession

This old man

English traditional

Round go the mill wheels

French traditional

One player only

Everyone together

Song and dance

West Indian traditional

Solo Tutti Solo

Tutti Solo Tutti

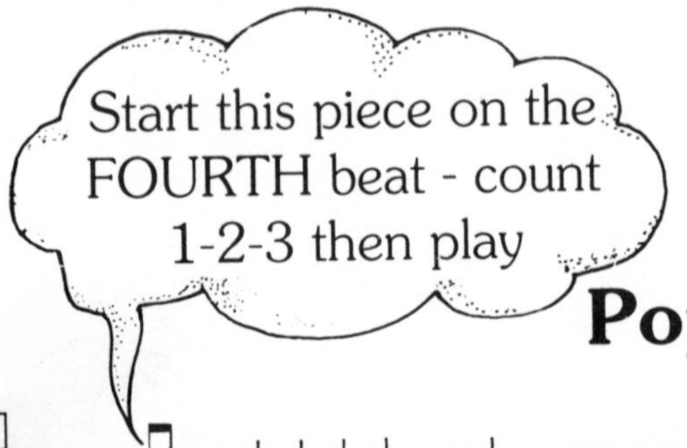

Solo Tutti

Start this piece on the FOURTH beat - count 1-2-3 then play

Popular song

American traditional

Twinkle, twinkle little star

Traditional

'Swops'

Duet

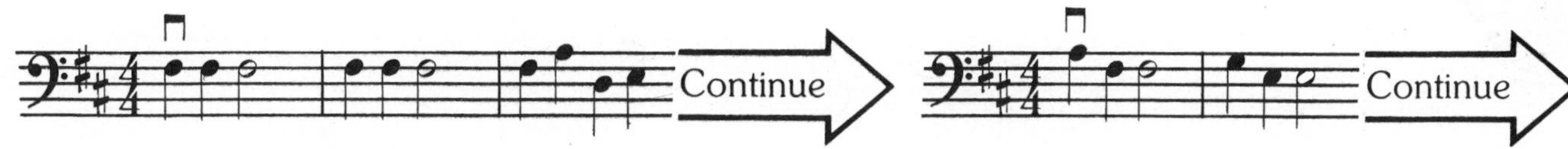

The note C

Slow march

GORDON BANON

Russian lullaby

Okushiri

Japanese traditional

Kol dodi

Jewish traditional

Chanson

Eliza

Past three o'clock

English traditional carol

Oranges and lemons

English traditional

London's burning

Round

English traditional

Ye banks and braes

Scottish traditional

QUAVER rest
A handsome lad
Irish traditional
Lively
Up bow
Congratulations
Words and Music by
BILL MARTIN and PHIL COULTER
Happily
D7
G
A7
Am7
D7
G
G♯o
D7/A
D7
G
A7
Am7
D7
G
Minuet
WOLFGANG AMADEUS MOZART
(1756-1791)
Moderately

Mongoose
Brightly
Jamaican traditional
Up bow
The prospector
Steadily
American traditional
Schottisch
FRANZ SCHUBERT
(1797-1828)
Simply
Now we are met
Slowly
Duet

Dotted crotchets

4
4
Clap, say, and play the rhythm

Michael row the boat ashore

Moderately

Spiritual

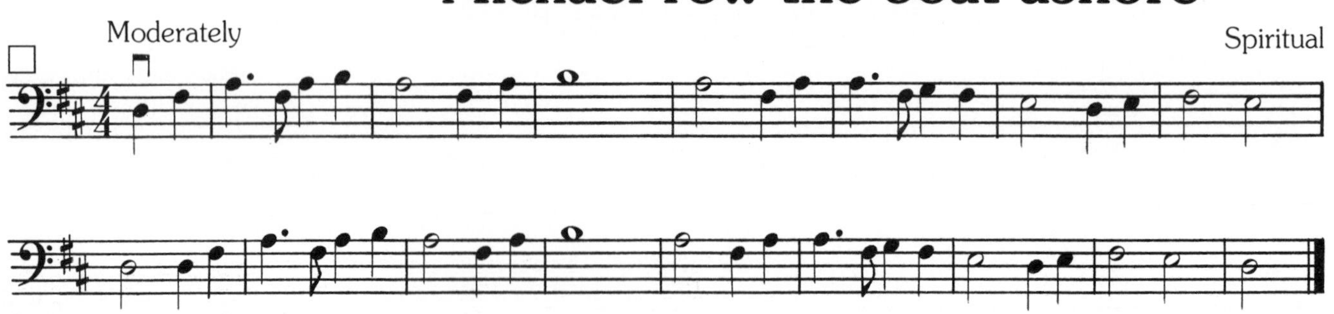

The muffin man

English traditional

Rhythmically

Village song

Not too fast

Peruvian traditional

THREE MINIM
BEATS in each bar
Kum ba yah
Spiritual
Joyfully
1.

Joyfully
2.

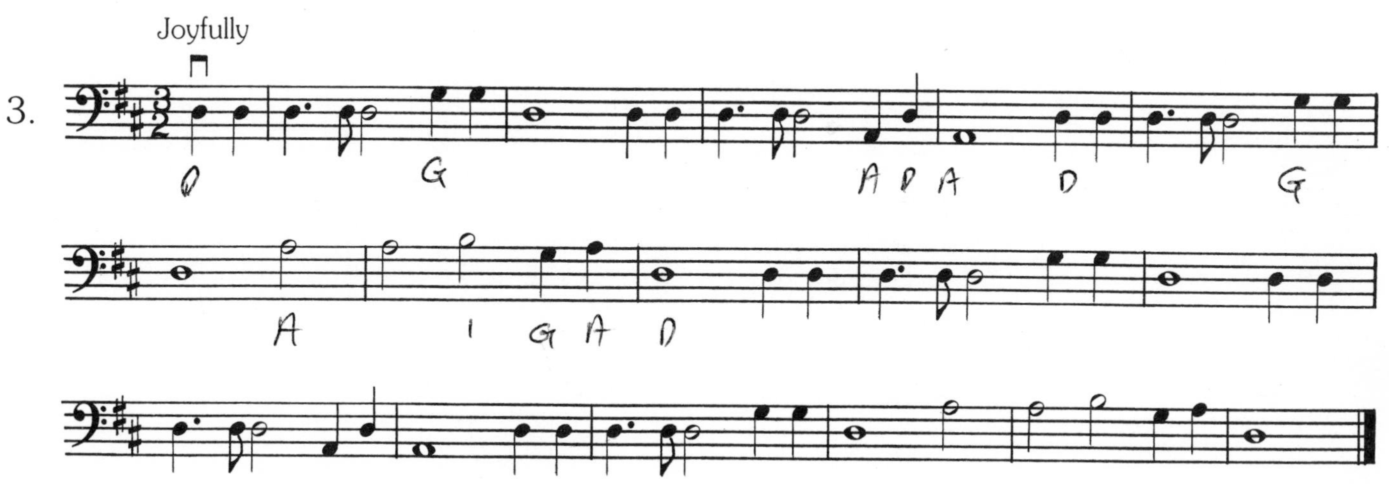
Joyfully
3.

Edelweiss

Lyrics by OSCAR HAMMERSTEIN II
Music by RICHARD RODGERS

From *The Sound of Music*

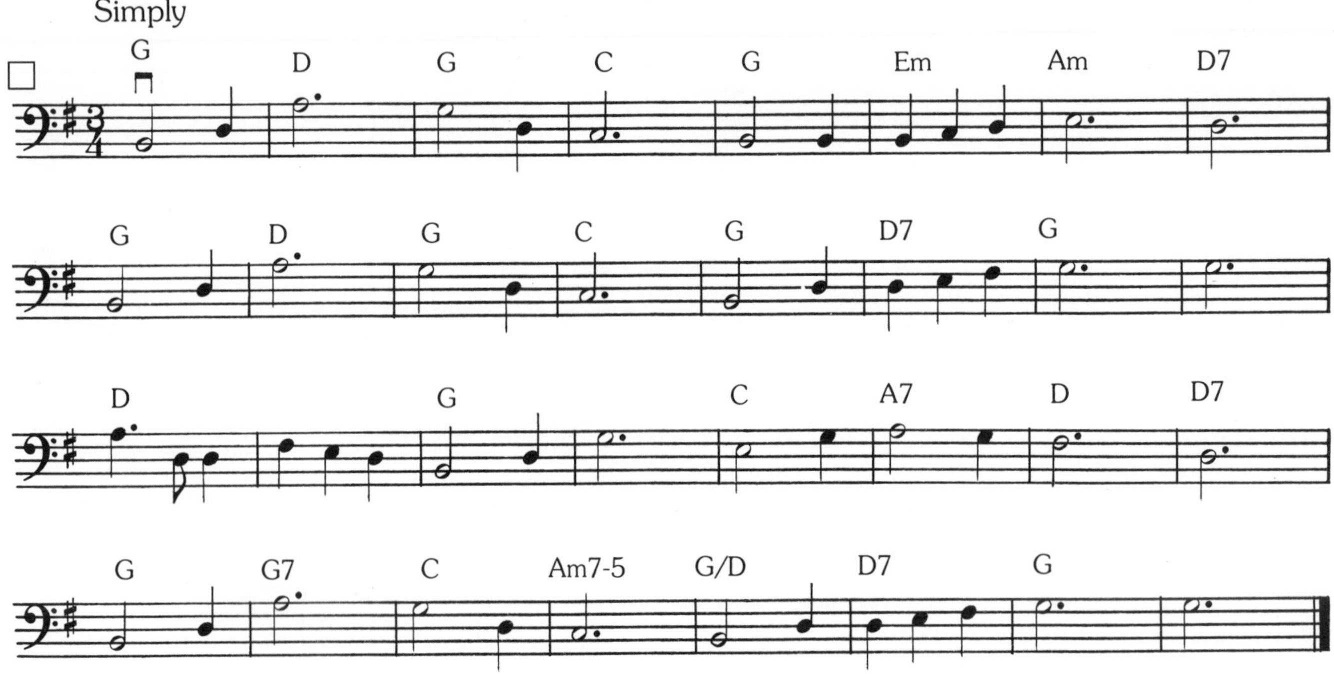

London bridge

English traditional

Donkey riding

Traditional

Double Bass solo

From the *First Symphony*

GUSTAV MAHLER
(1860-1911)

Like a funeral march

Loch Lomond

Simply

Scottish traditional

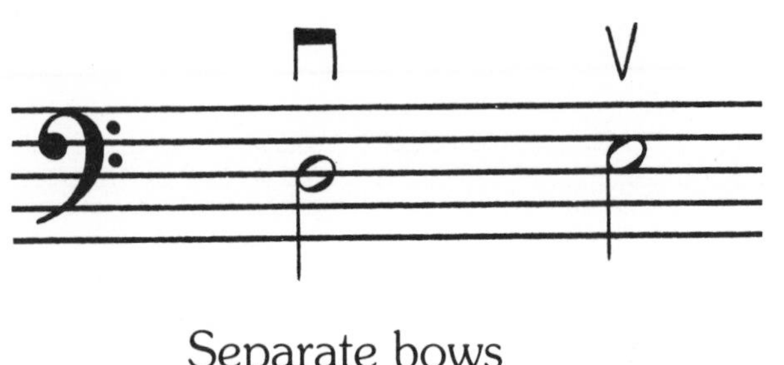

Separate bows

Slur

Etude 1

Etude 2

Ode to joy

From the Ninth Symphony

LUDWIG VAN BEETHOVEN
(1770-1827)

Majestically

The wizard

1st and 2nd-time bars

The nightingale

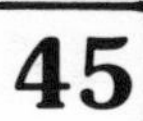

Jingle bells

Presto

American traditional

The first Nowell

Joyfully

(Accompaniment)

English traditional carol

O come, all ye faithful

Moderato

(Accompaniment)

J.F. WADE (1711-1786)

O little town of Bethlehem

Moderato

(Accompaniment)

English traditional carol

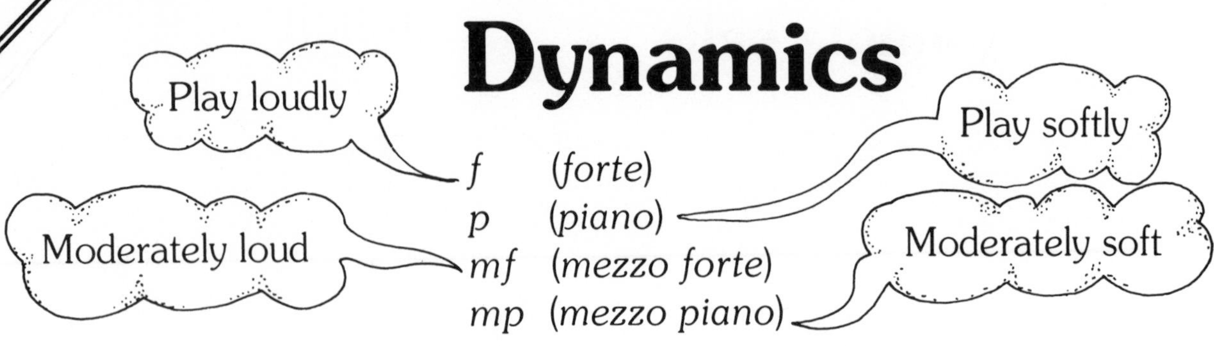

Allegretto

f *p* *f* *p*

f *p* *f* *p*

Frère Jacques

French traditional

Brightly

Round

(1) (2) (3) (4)

f *p* *f* *p* *f* *p* *f* *p*

The willow tree

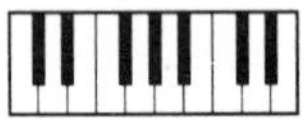

Flowing

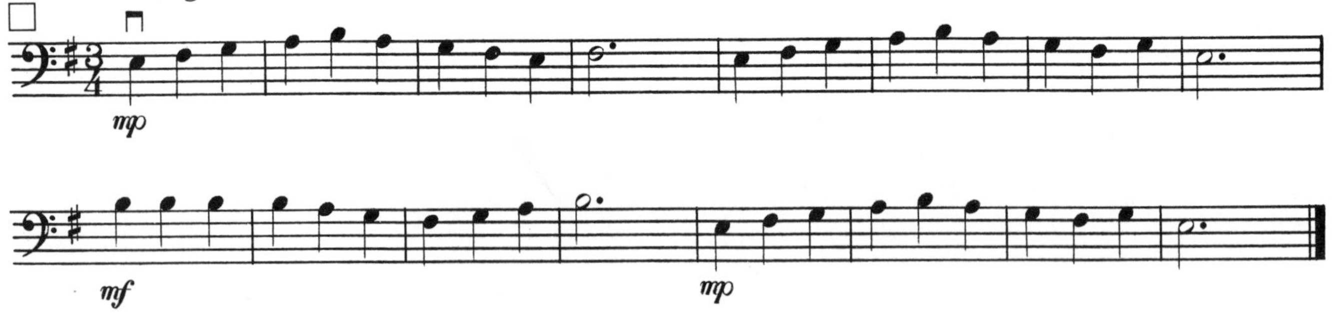

mp

mf *mp*

Pattern

Moderato

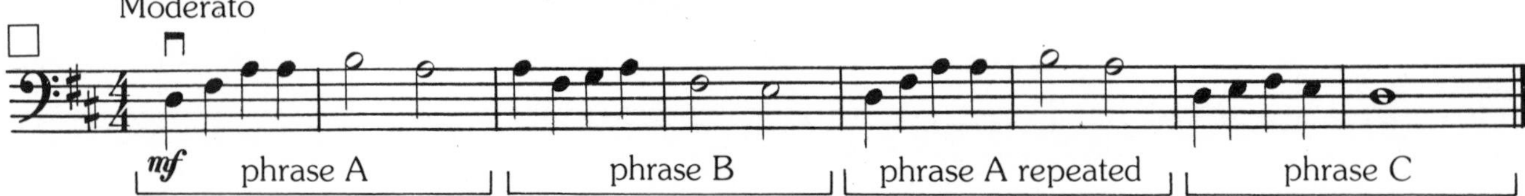

Compose a piece with the same structure as 'Pattern'

Tied notes

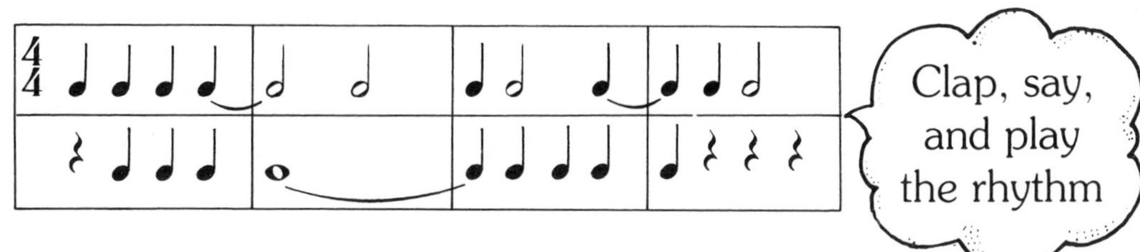

Clap, say, and play the rhythm

A minimim tied to a crotchet lasts for 3 beats

A crotchet tied to a crotchet lasts for 2 beats

A semibreve tied to a crotchet lasts for 5 beats, and so on

Up bow

When the saints go marching in

Up bow

Old Texas

Syncopation

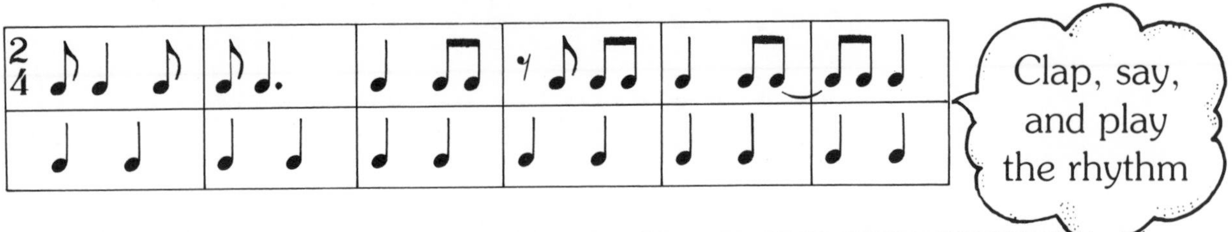

Clap, say, and play the rhythm

The rolling heather

Moderato

Scottish traditional

p

Twelve bar blues

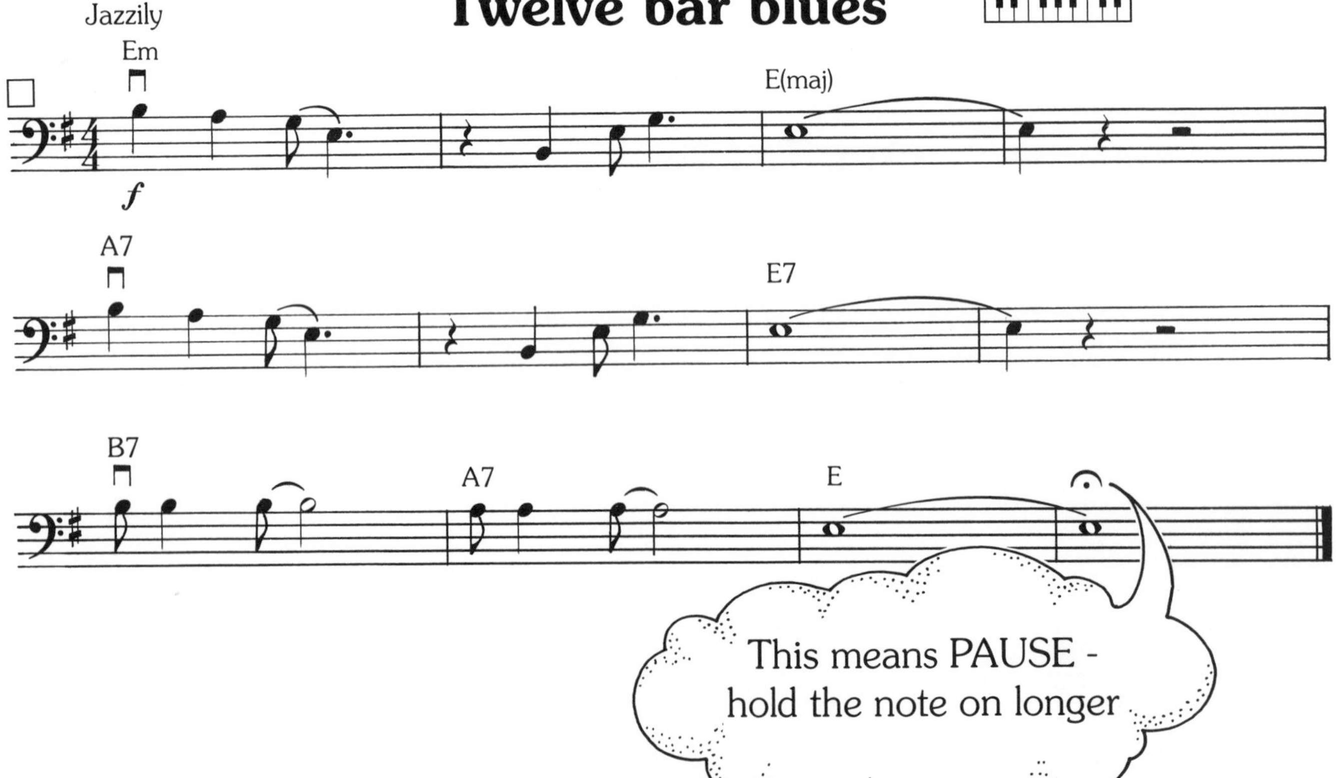

Jazzily

Em

f

E(maj)

A7

E7

B7

A7

E

This means PAUSE - hold the note on longer

Jamaican dance

Traditional

Lambeth walk

Words and Music by NOEL GAY
and DOUGLAS FURBER

Sam's piece

Composed by thirteen-year old Sam Wilkinson

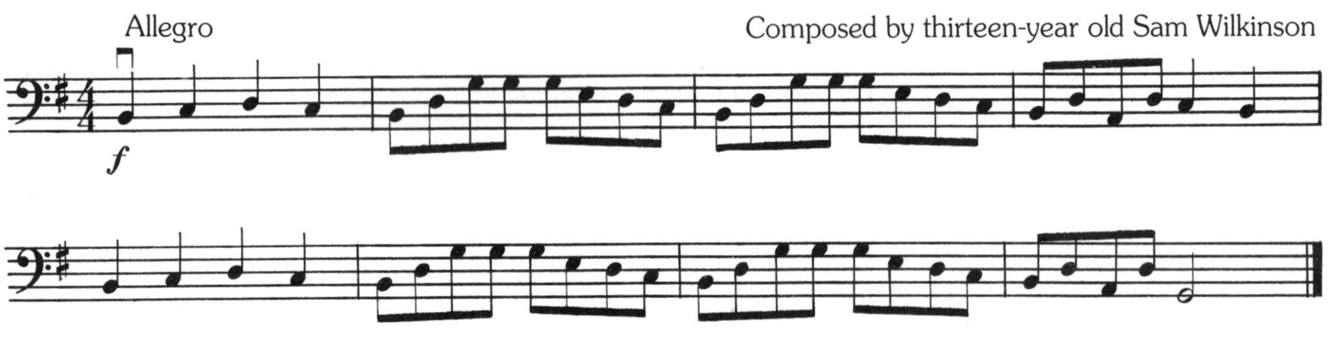

The white cliffs of Dover

(Accompaniment)

Words by WALTER KENT
Music by NAT BURTON

Sentimentally

A7 D *pizz.* F♯m D7 G G♯° D/A Bm Em7

mf

A A7 D Bm Em7 A7 D F♯m D7

G G♯° D/A Bm Em7 A A7 D G

D D7 G G+ Em/G G♯° D/A D D7 G Em

f

Bm Bm E7 Em7 A7 D F♯m D7

mf

G G♯° D/A Bm Em7 A A7 D B♭ D

All night, all day

Spiritual

52
In 5/4 time each bar adds up to five crotchet beats
The clowns
Composed by thirteen-year old Collette Cassidy
Giocoso
Fine
f
D.C. al Fine
I gave my love a cherry
Traditional
Andante cantabile
mf
Passion chorale
JOHANN SEBASTIAN BACH
(1685-1750)
Religioso
mp

Old Macdonald

Traditional

Top C in second position

Valse

Yankee Doodle

American traditional

The grand old Duke of York

English traditional

Summer song

Czech traditional

Top D in third position

Lullaby

Duet

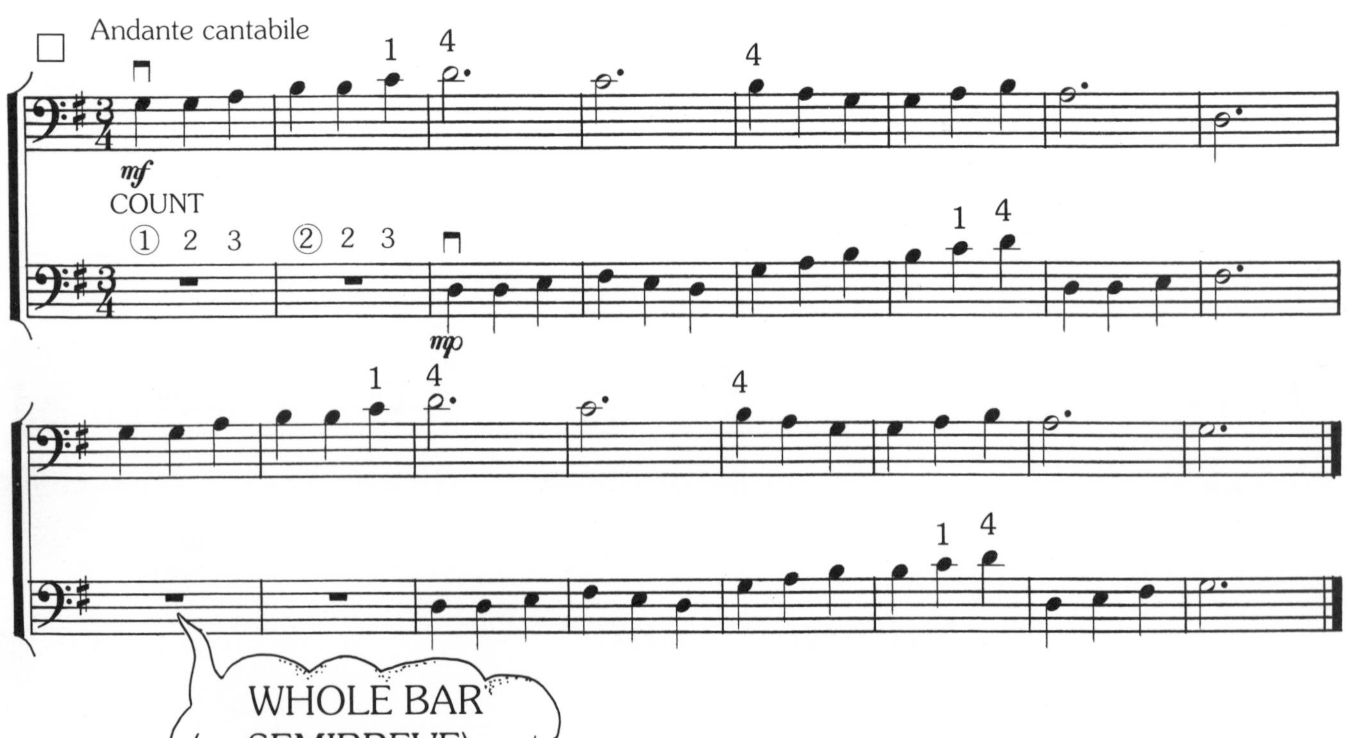

Good King Wenceslas

English traditional carol

Accidentals

The SHARP raises the pitch of a note by ONE SEMITONE

The carousel

Smoothly

mf

The NATURAL sign cancels the effect of the F sharp in the key signature

Hymn tune

Slowly

mp

St. Anthony Chorale

JOSEPH HAYDN
(1732-1809)

Moderato

Duet

mf

Fine

mp

D.C. al Fine

The CAUTIONARY ACCIDENTAL reminds you this note is C and no longer C♯

$\frac{6}{8}$ time

and its relationship with $\frac{2}{4}$ time.

Semiquavers

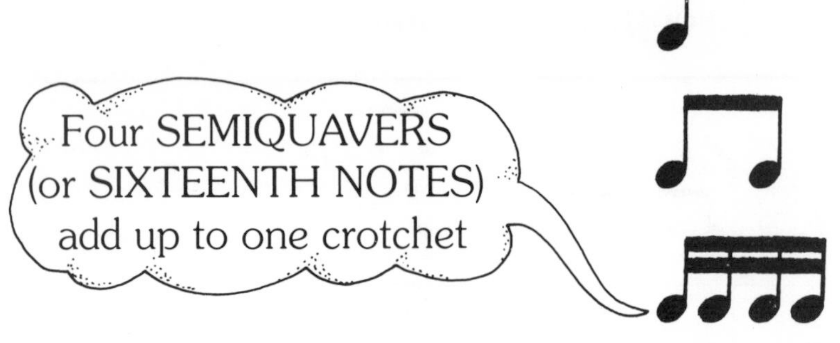

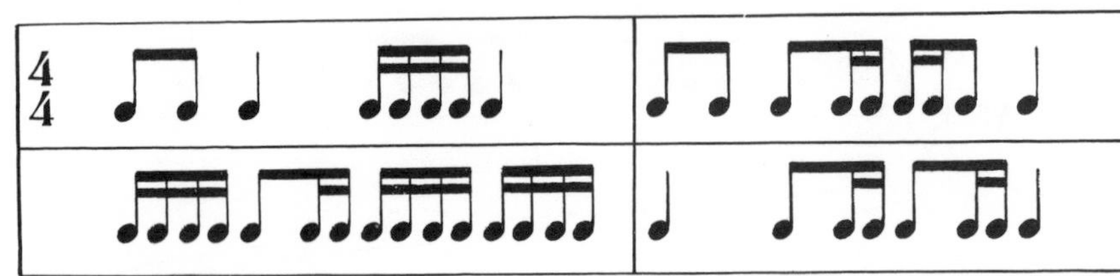

Clap, say, and play the rhythm

Semiquaver study

Gallop

JACQUES OFFENBACH (1819-1880)

From the opera *Orpheus in the Underworld*

Dotted quavers

Clap, say, and play the rhythm

Happy birthday to you

Words and Music by
PATTY S. HILL and MILDRED HILL

Moderato

D7 G B♭° D7/A D7 G

G C Am7 G/D D7 G

Oh Susannah

American traditional

Up bow
Brightly

Chitty Chitty Bang Bang

Words and Music by
RICHARD SHERMAN and ROBERT SHERMAN

Scarboro' fair

Traditional

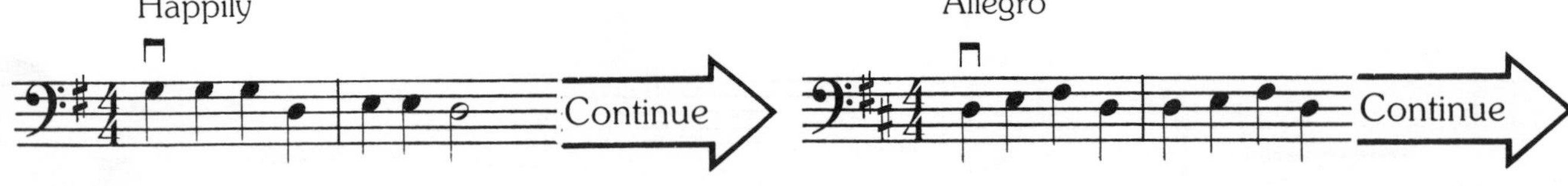

The QUAVER TRIPLET means that three quavers are played in the time of one crotchet
Amazing grace
Traditional
Slowly
1.
mp
3
3
3
3
Slowly
2.
mp
2nd finger
Slowly
pizz.
3.
mp

Slurring three notes to a bow

Ruthin gardens

Austrian song

Silent night

FRANZ GRUBER
(1787-1863)

The Skye boat song 

Scottish traditional

1.

Smoothly

mf

f

Fine

D. C. al Fine
(no repeat)

rit.

RIT. (ritardando) means 'slowing down'

2.

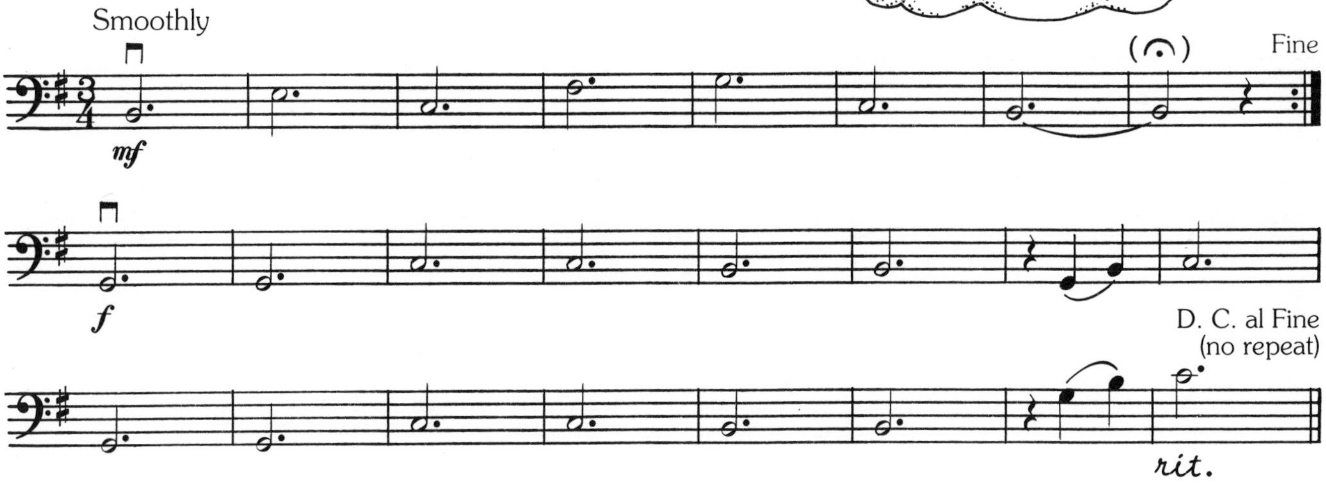

Smoothly

mf

f

Fine

D. C. al Fine
(no repeat)

rit.

Scales and arpeggios

G major

C major

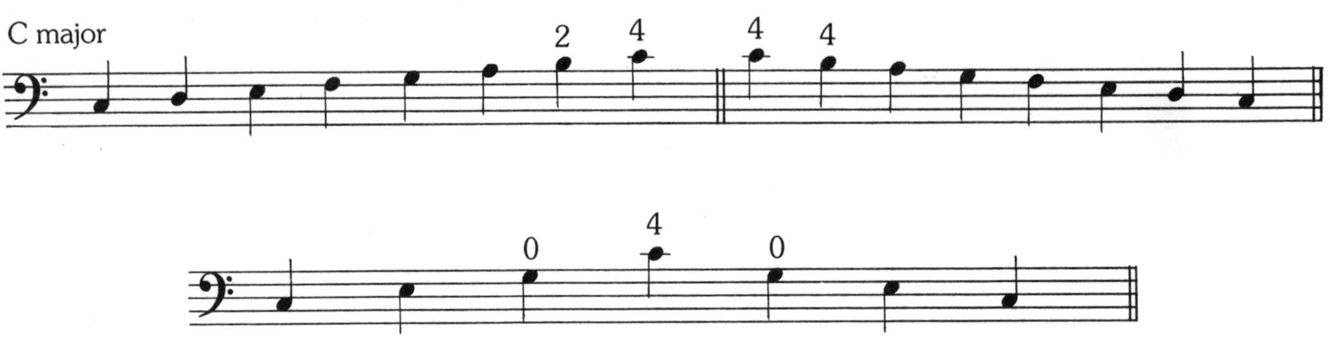

D major

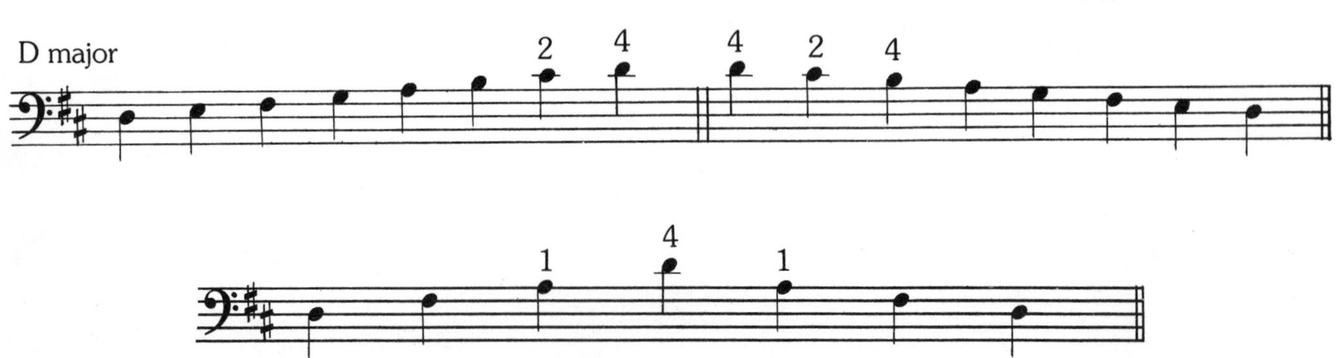